The Alphabet - 2
M - Z

The monkey sits on a mushroom under the moon.

Student Reader
Practice Book
Teacher Guide

Learning English Curriculum
Since 1999
www.efl-esl.com

Learning English Curriculum

Copyright © 2023 ALL RIGHTS RESERVED.

You are permitted to print or photocopy as many copies as you need for your school. Online distribution is not permitted. Please contact us if you wish to teach online.

Re-Sales is not permitted.

Notice: Learning English Curriculum makes every reasonable effort to obtain from reliable sources accurate, complete, and timely information about the tests covered in this book. Nevertheless, changes can be made in the tests or the administration of the tests at any time and Learning English Curriculum makes no representation or warranty, either expressed or implied as to the accuracy, timeliness, or completeness of the information contained in this book.

Learning English Curriculum make no representations or warranties of any kind, express or implied, about the completeness, accuracy, reliability, suitability or availability with respect to the information contained in this document for any purpose. Any reliance you place on such information is therefore strictly at your own risk.

The author(s) shall not be liable for any loss incurred as a consequence of the use and application, directly or indirectly, of any information presented in this work. Sold with the understanding, the author is not engaged in rendering professional services or advice. If advice or expert assistance is required, the services of a competent professional should be sought.

Published by:
Learning English Curriculum
Visit us online
https://www.efl-esl.com

ISBN: 9781772454048

Printing this Document

This file contains 3 books - to print:

Student reader - Pages 1 - 47
Student Workbook - Pages 48 - 76
Teacher Guide - Pages - 77 - 101

The **STUDENT BOOK** that accompanies this guide is written for children under the age of seven. The large print text containing the key words for the letter being introduced will introduce the children to reading. Reading expectations will vary according to the age of the children. Some will start to read, while many will need to participate in the activities and exercises provided. However, the sentences provided on the pages should be read to the children and repeated by the children a number of times. We suggest that the children place a marker under each sentence as they repeat it.

Adapt the instructions for all pages to meet the needs of your students.

Children learn their first language by listening and repeating what they hear. It is important that they have many opportunities to listen to and repeat the English sentences. Although many animals and birds are shown and used as examples of initial letter sounds, the children will not memorize the names of all of these. We suggest that during the listening exercises only, the teacher stress the first sound of each word. Explain that each letter has a name, just as they have names.

The basic teacher instructions are given in the small boxes on each page. This is efficient for the teacher and also allows the parents to understand what the child has been asked to do

It will be important to provide the students with paper markers of about 17 centimeters long and 5 centimeters wide. These are attractive if they are made of colored paper or cardboard. Having a class set of laminated markers saves time and money.

When the children count it helps them if that they touch the person, object or picture as they count. They should move in a left to right direction. Although most children of three and four will not be able to do this without help, it will lead them to understand the concept of a one to one relationship.

The **PRACTICE BOOK** provides independent work for the children. They will need a brief explanation of what they are to do before starting the pages that accompany each lesson. A brief review of how to form the large letters will ensure that they practice the movements correctly when using a crayon. A pencil can be used when printing between the lines.

Adapt the instructions for all pages to meet the needs of your students.

The **TEACHER'S GUIDE** includes games that provide essential listening and speaking experiences. We suggest that these activities and games be saved for the latter part of the class when the children are tired. It has been our experience that when the children arrive, the first thing they ask is, "Can we play a game now?' or "Can we play Bingo now"? Our answer was to tell them that there is work we need to do first, so let's get busy so we can play a game or two. We found that they developed a positive attitude towards learning English. This allowed everyone to enjoy the class time.
These games reinforce the lessons covered in the book. They are a very important part of the program.

Note: You are the teacher – do it your way!
We wish you success with your classes,
Daisy Stocker B.Ed. M.Ed.   George Stocker D.D.S.

FROM - M to Z

STUDENT BOOK 1B

CONTENTS

VERSES

Lesson 13	Mm	Longlegs	39
Lesson 14	Nn	Longlegs	42
Lesson 15	Oo	Longlegs	45
Lesson 16	Pp	Longlegs	48
Lesson 17	Qq	Longlegs	51
Lesson 18	Rr	Longlegs	54
Lesson 19	Ss	Boats	57
Lesson 20	Tt	Boats	60
Lesson 21	Uu	Boats	63
Lesson 22	Vv	Boats	66
Lesson 23	Ww	Make Believe	69
Lesson 24	Xx	Make Believe	72
Lesson 25	Yy	Make Believe	75
Lesson 26	Zz	Make Believe	78

INDEX OF PHONICS
BOOK 1B
FROM - M TO Z

Saying Letter Names – 39, 42, 45, 48, 51, 54, 57, 60, 63, 66, 69, 72, 75, 78

Picture – Initial Sounds – 39, 42, 45, 48, 51, 54, 57, 60, 63, 66, 69, 72, 75, 78

Tracing/Printing Letters – 39, 42, 43, 45, 48, 51, 54, 57, 60, 64, 66, 69, 72, 75, 78,

Speaking – all pages

Counting – 40, 46

Identifying similarities and differences –40, 42, 43, 58, 70

Identifying beginning Consonants –43, 44, 50, 52, 55, 61, 64, 67, 70, 73, 76, 79

Following Oral Directions – all pages

Listening – all pages

Maze – 49, 74

Verses – 42, 44, 47, 50, 53, 56, 59, 62, 65, 68, 71, 74, 77, 80

The Alphabet 2 - Student Reader

LESSON 13

Objectives – to teach: the symbol and sound for Mm – identifying the initial Mm in words – vocabulary – sentence structure – sentence comprehension - identifying visual differences – identifying auditory differences – following oral directions – counting to ten – reading numbers to 10 – listening to a story –

Put your finger on the big "M".
Put your finger on the little "m".

Print big "M" with your crayon. Start at the top and go down.
Print little "m" with your crayon.

Put your finger on the monkey. **Say:** monkey. Stress the first sound.
Put your finger on the mushrooms.
Do you like mushrooms?

Put your finger on the moon.
Put your finger on the moon's nose.
Put your finger on the moon's mouth.

The monkey sits on a mushroom under the moon.

Print the big "M's" with your crayon. Start at the top and go down.

Print the little "m's" with your crayon.

The Alphabet 2 - Student Reader

LESSON 13 CONTINUED

Circle the mushroom that is different.				

Circle the moon that is different.				

Have the children point to the pictures as you say: boy, mother, moon, girl, monkey. Circle the pictures that start with **Mm**.					

The children point to the pictures as you say: moon, frog, mushroom, mother, insect. Circle the pictures that begin with **Mm**.					

Count the fingers in the picture. Start at "1" and put your finger on each number as you count. Numbers "1" and "10" are thumbs. Color the thumbs pink.

Count the fingers on your friend's hands. Touch each finger as you count.

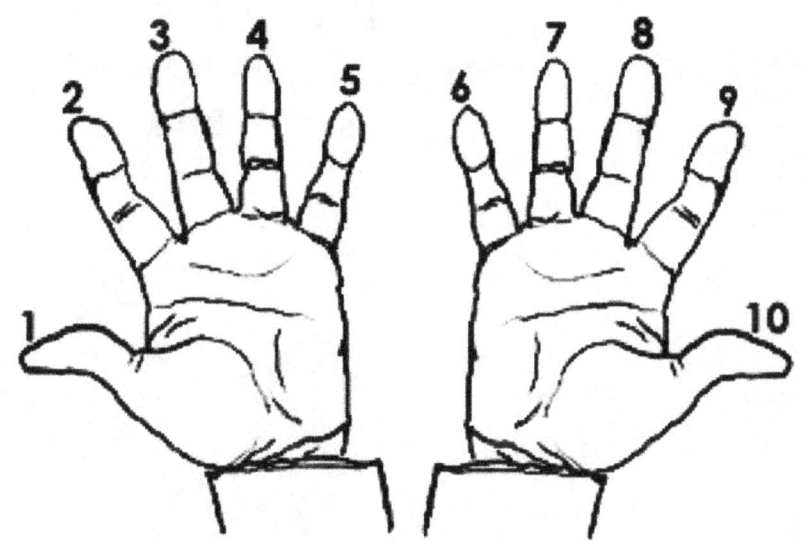

The Alphabet 2 - Student Reader

LESSON 13 CONTINUED

LONGLEGS
Once upon a time a girl and a boy
made a puppet named Longlegs.
When Longlegs got his jacket and pants and shoes,
he started to run.
As Longlegs ran he called:

I can run
It's lots of fun.
You can't catch me
Because I'm free.

To the teacher:
Read the story several times. Have the children point to Longlegs standing, Longlegs running, his jacket, pants and shoes. Have them say what Longlegs calls several times. They are not expected to memorize it, but they will learn it as it is repeated in the next verses.

Put your finger on each picture and say:
Longlegs, boy, pony.
Circle the ones that are running.

The Alphabet 2 - Student Reader

LESSON 14

Objectives – to teach: the symbol and sound for Nn – identifying the initial Nn in words – vocabulary – sentence structure – sentence comprehension - identifying visual differences – identifying auditory differences – following oral directions – reviewing a story - understanding a story – repeating story parts.

To the teacher: The narwhale is a mammal that lives in the Arctic seas. Say: Put your finger on the narwhale. It lives in the cold water. Say narwhale. Print big "N". Start at the top. Print little "n". Color the narwhale's fin.

The narwhale has a long nose!

Print the big "N's" with your yellow crayon Start at the top.

N N N N

Print the small "n's".

n n n n

Circle the narwhale that is different. Color all the fins.

LESSON 14 CONTINUED

Put your finger on the nest as you say "nest". Repeat for: tree, bird, eggs.

How many eggs do you see?

The bird has a nest in the tree.

Put your finger on each letter as you say its name. Circle the letter that is different.

n m n n

Put your finger on each letter and say its name. Circle the letter that is different.

i j i i i

Put your finger on: necklace, kettle, narwhale. Circle the pictures that start with "**Nn**".

Put your finger on: fish, nest, monkey, necklace. Circle the pictures that start with "**Nn**".

The Alphabet 2 - Student Reader

LESSON 14 CONTINUED

To the teacher: Read the story from Page 41 and have the children say Longlegs' verse with you before reading this page. Have the children put their fingers on the clown, his hat, his shoes and his arms. Then, on Longlegs' pants, jacket, arms, mouth and knees.
Ask: Do you like to run? Are Longlegs' knees like yours? Will the clown catch Longlegs.

**Longlegs ran and ran until a funny clown tried to catch him.
As Longlegs ran he called:
"I can run
It's lots of fun.
You can't catch me
Because I'm free."**

Put your finger on each picture and say: nest, lantern, kite, mushrooms, narwhale, necklace.

Draw a line to the "Nn" from each picture that starts with **Nn**.

44
The Alphabet 2 - Student Reader

LESSON 15

Objectives – to teach: the symbol and short sound for Oo – identifying the initial short Oo in words – vocabulary – sentence structure – sentence comprehension - identifying visual differences – identifying auditory differences – following oral directions – reviewing the first stories - listening to and saying story verses - new story - printing.

To the teacher: The octopus has tube feet on its legs so it can cling to the rocks. One leg shows the tube feet.
Say octopus. Put your finger on big "O", say its name.
Print big "O" with your crayon. Start at the top.
Print little "o" with your crayon.
Put your finger on the octopus.
Say:
"The octopus lives in the sea."
Color the leg that looks different.
Color its eye.

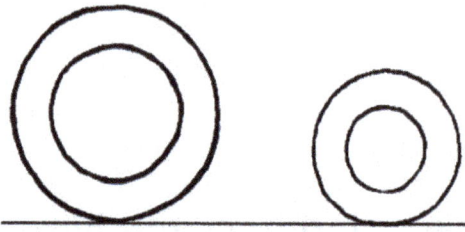

The octopus lives in the sea.

Print the big "O's" with your crayon. Start at the top.

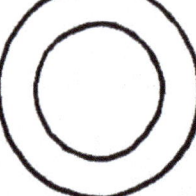 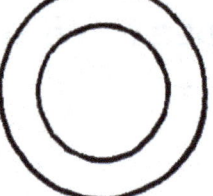 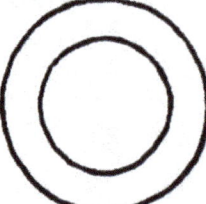 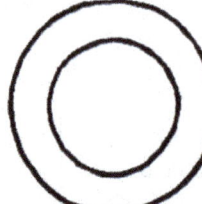

Print the small "o's" with your crayon.

   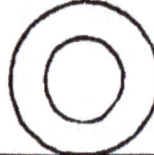

Say: octopus, necklace, osprey. Circle the ones that start with **Oo**. Color the osprey's tail.

The Alphabet 2 - Student Reader

LESSON 15 CONTINUED

Animals and birds that live at the pond.

Have the children point to the animals and birds and say their names:
frogs, bird, nest, osprey, octopus, otter, fish.
Say:
Put your finger on the pond.
Put your fingers on the two frogs and color them green.
Put your finger on the bird's nest and color the eggs blue.

Color the osprey's tail.
Color the octopus red because it is angry.
Color the tree brown.

Draw a blue circle around the fish.
Draw a yellow circle around the otter with a fish in its mouth.

Circle the bird that is different. Color its beak.

Put your finger on the otter.
What is in the otter's mouth?
Do you eat fish?
Color the otter's long tail.

Put your finger on the octopus.
Count its legs.
How many legs does it have?

The Alphabet 2 - Student Reader

LESSON 15 CONTINUED

**So Longlegs ran and ran until a big dog tried to catch him.
As Longlegs ran he called:**

I can run
It's lots of fun.
You can't catch me
Because I'm free.

To the teacher: Read the stories from Pages 41 and 44 to the children, having them say Longlegs' words with you. Then have them repeat dog, jacket, pants, shoes, knees, as they point to each of those items on this page.
Ask: What is the dog doing? What is Longlegs doing?
Is Longlegs a puppet? Do you have a puppet?

Circle the smallest O.

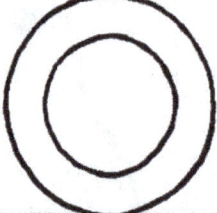 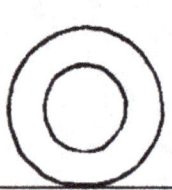 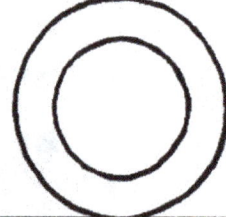 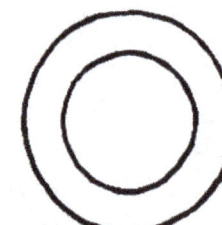

Circle the ones that can run like you and me.

The Alphabet 2 - Student Reader

LESSON 16

Objectives – to teach: the symbol and sound for Pp – identifying the initial Pp in words – vocabulary – sentence structure – sentence comprehension - identifying visual differences – identifying auditory differences – following oral directions – reviewing the first three stories- listening to and saying story verses – new story - printing.

Put your finger on the big "P". Say P.
Put your finger on the little "P"
Put your finger on the mother panda.
Say "panda" stressing the first sound.
Put your finger on the baby panda.
Put your finger on the tree.

Say: "Pandas live in the trees."
Print big "P" with your crayon. Start at the top and then go around.
Print little "p".
Color the baby panda's tummy.

The pandas live in the trees.

Print the big "P's" with your crayon.

P   P   P   P

Print the little "p's" with your crayon.

p   p   p   p

Say: panda, goat, pelican.
Circle the ones that start with Pp.
Color the pelican's beak.

The Alphabet 2 - Student Reader

LESSON 16 CONTINUED

Say: Ride the pony to the zoo. Don't let the ghost catch you.

Put your finger on the bird with the longest beak.
Color its beak.
Draw a circle around the smallest bird.
Color the bird with the open beak.

Have the children put their fingers on the pictures as they say: pig, pony, ball. Circle the ones that start with Pp.

  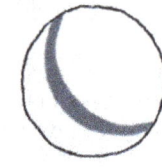

The Alphabet 2 - Student Reader

LESSON 16 CONTINUED

To the teacher: Read the stories on Pages 41, 44 and 47 before you read this, having the children say Longlegs' words with you. While reading the above story, encourage them to say any of the words with you. Read it several times. Have the children put their fingers on the following as you say: dragon, tongue, smoke, tail. Then: Longlegs, knees, shoes, pants, jacket, mouth.
Have them color items that they don't know well. **Ask:** Can a dragon catch you? Is it fun to run?

**So Longlegs ran and ran until a dragon tried to catch him.
As Longlegs ran he called:**

**I can run
It's lots of fun.
You can't catch me
Because I'm free.**

The Alphabet 2 - Student Reader

LESSON 17

Objectives – to teach: the symbol and sound for Qq – identifying the initial Qq in words – vocabulary – sentence structure – sentence comprehension - identifying visual differences – identifying auditory differences – following oral directions – reviewing the story - listening to, saying and understanding the new story -- printing.

Put your finger on big "Q". Say Q. Print it with your crayon. Make the circle first.
Print little "q" with your crayon. Make the circle first.

Put your finger on the Queen. Say "Queen" stressing the first sound.
Put your finger on the ducks.
What do they say?
How many ducks do you see?

Have the children repeat, "The Queen is feeding the ducks." several times.

Make the Queen's robe red and white.
Color her arms pink.

The queen is feeding the ducks.

Print the big "Q's" with your crayon. Make the circle first, then draw the line.

Print the little "q's" with your crayon. Make the circle first.

Say: queen, quail, hat. Circle the ones that start with Qq.

The Alphabet 2 - Student Reader

LESSON 17 CONTINUED

To the teacher: Have the children point to and say the letter names. Then point to and say: elephant, goat, apple, boy, cat, hat, dinosaur, frog. They are to match the beginning sound and the letter.

Aa
Bb
Cc
Dd
Ee
Ff
Gg
Hh

The Alphabet 2 - Student Reader

LESSON 17 CONTINUED

To the teacher: Review the stories on Pages 41, 44, 47 and 50 encouraging the children to say the words with you. Read this story, pointing out the difference in the verse.
Say: Put your fingers on two girl puppets. Put your fingers on two boy puppets. Put your fingers on the girl's dresses, on their long hair, on their shoes. Put your finger on an elbow.
Color Longlegs' three friends. **Ask:** Do you have friends? Do you have long hair?

Longlegs ran and ran until he met some puppet friends. As Longlegs ran he called:

Run, run
It's lots of fun.
If you run with me
We'll all be free.

So the puppets ran with Longlegs.

Say: monkey, osprey, moon. Circle the ones that start with "**Mm**".

Say: mushrooms, nest, necklace. Circle the ones that start with "**Nn**".

The Alphabet 2 - Student Reader

LESSON 18

Objectives – to teach: the symbol and sound for Rr – identifying the initial Rr in words – vocabulary – sentence structure – sentence comprehension - identifying visual differences – identifying auditory differences – following oral directions – reviewing the story - listening to, saying and understanding the final part of the story –- printing.

Rr

Cock-a-doodle-doo
Good morning to you.

To the teacher: Put your finger on the big "R", its name is R. Repeat for small r. Have the children print the letters starting at the top. Put your finger on the rooster and say "rooster". Repeat for rabbit. Read the caption and have the children repeat it several times. **Say:** The rooster says "Cock-a-doodle-doo" in the morning when the sun comes up. Color the rabbit's ears brown.

| Put your finger on big R, say its name and print it with your crayon. | R | R | R | R |

| Put your finger on little r, say its name and print it with your crayon. | r | r | r | r |

The Alphabet 2 - Student Reader

LESSON 18 CONTINUED

Say: rooster, kettle, rabbit. Circle the ones that start with Rr.

Say the names as you put your finger on the goat and rhinoceros. Put your finger on the goat's horns. They are behind its ears. Put your finger on the rhinoceros' horn. Its horn is on its nose. Put your finger on your nose.
Ask: Do you have a horn on your nose? Color the goat's horns. Color the rhinoceros' horn.

Circle the one that is different.

 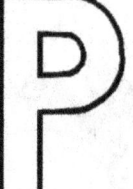  

To the teacher: Have the children point as they name the animals – pig, lion, rabbit, rooster, kangaroos, rhinoceros. Color the ones that start with Rr.

The Alphabet 2 - Student Reader

LESSON 18 CONTINUED

**They all ran and ran.
They ran to the girl and boy who made Longlegs.**

They all called: **It's lots of fun
To run and run.
Please come and play
With us today.**

To the teacher: Read the first part to the children and help them understand where the puppets are going. **Ask**: What are the puppets doing? How many girl puppets? How many boy puppets? Color the puppet's legs.
Read the last part of the story and have the children repeat it several times. **Say:** Put your finger on the boy. Put your finger on the girl. Put your finger on the puppet's knees. Put your finger on the puppet's elbows. Color the puppet's dresses. Color the puppet's pants.

LESSON 19

Objectives – to teach: the symbol and sound for Ss – identifying the initial Ss in words – vocabulary – sentence structure – sentence comprehension - identifying visual differences – identifying auditory differences – following oral directions – introducing a story - listening to and saying a new verse –- printing.

Put your finger on the big "S". Say its name. Repeat for little "s". Print big S and little s starting at the top.

Put your finger on the spider. Have the children say "spider" stressing the first sound.

The spider made a web in the tree.

Put your finger on big S. Print the big "S's" with your crayon.

Put your finger on little s. Print the little "s's" with your crayon.

Say: spider, rooster, scissors. Circle the ones that start with Ss.

The Alphabet 2 - Student Reader

LESSON 19 CONTINUED

Sea Animals

To the teacher: Tell the children that the sea lion lives on the rocks beside the sea and likes to swim with the octopuses and the fishes. Have them put their finger on the sea, the sea lion, the octopus and the fishes.
Do the sea lion's feet look like your feet? Its feet are called flippers. Put your finger on the flippers.
Color the fishes blue and yellow.

Put your finger on "S". Put your finger on "3". Circle the one that is different.				
Circle the spider that is different.				

The Alphabet 2 - Student Reader

LESSON 19 CONTINUED

BOATS

My plastic boat
that's blue and red
It always sits
beside my bed.

My boats are here,
My boats are there,
My little boats are everywhere.

To the teacher: Ask the children if they have a toy boat. Read the verses. Have the children repeat them several times. Say: These are bunk beds. Put your finger on the top bed – on the bottom bed. Which bed would you like? Put your finger on the boat. Color its sails red. Put your finger on the boy. Color the boy's shirt green. Put your finger on the picture of the sea animals. Color the fishes. Teach the meaning of "here" and "there".

Look at each boat. Circle the sailboat that is different.

Circle the fishes.

Print the letters that are the same.

The Alphabet 2 - Student Reader

LESSON 20

Objectives – to teach: the symbol and sound for Tt – identifying the initial Tt in words – vocabulary – sentence structure – sentence comprehension - identifying visual differences – identifying auditory differences – following oral directions – reviewing a story - listening to and saying a new verse –- printing.

Will the turtle catch the tiger?

To the teacher: Put your finger on big "T" and have the children say its name. Print it starting at the top. Put your finger on little "t" and print it. Tell the children that the tiger and the turtle are having a race. Say: Put your finger on the turtle. Say turtle. Put your finger on the tiger. Put your finger on the trees. Read the question and ask what they think. Have the children say, turtle, tiger, tree as they point to each one. Color the turtle's back.
Ask: Which animal has the longest tail? Could you catch the turtle? Could you catch the tiger?

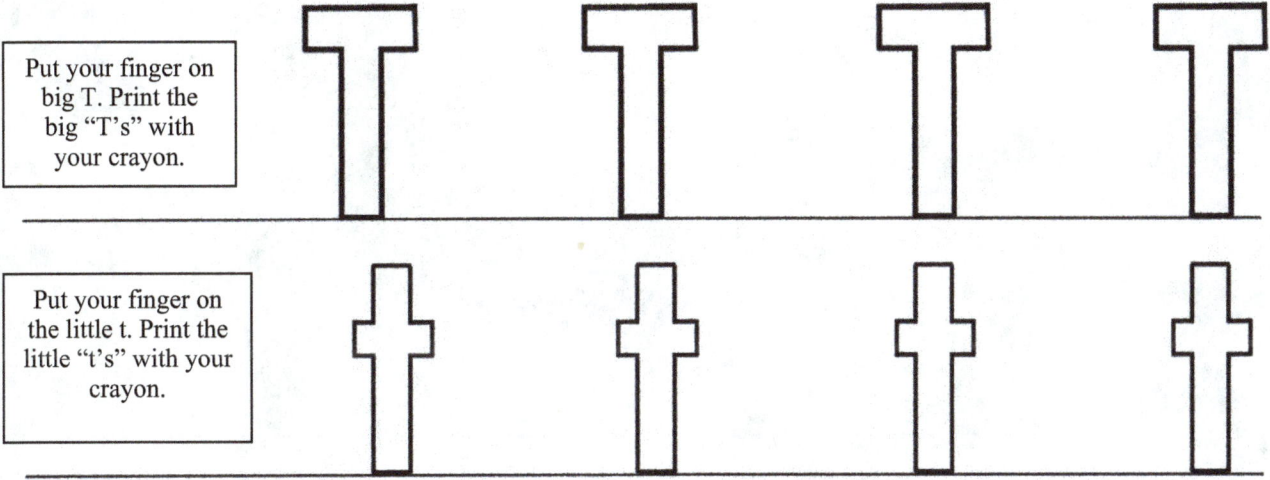

Put your finger on big T. Print the big "T's" with your crayon.

Put your finger on the little t. Print the little "t's" with your crayon.

The Alphabet 2 - Student Reader

LESSON 20 CONTINUED

To the teacher: Have the children put their finger on each letter and say its name – Bb, Gg, Jj, Ll, Mm, Tt, Ss, Rr. Repeat saying the other names – rabbit, monkey, boy, scissors, lantern, jacket, girl, tiger. The children are to draw a line from each letter to the picture that starts with that sound. For further review have them follow directions such as: "Color the girl's pants blue." Or "Color the monkey's feet brown."

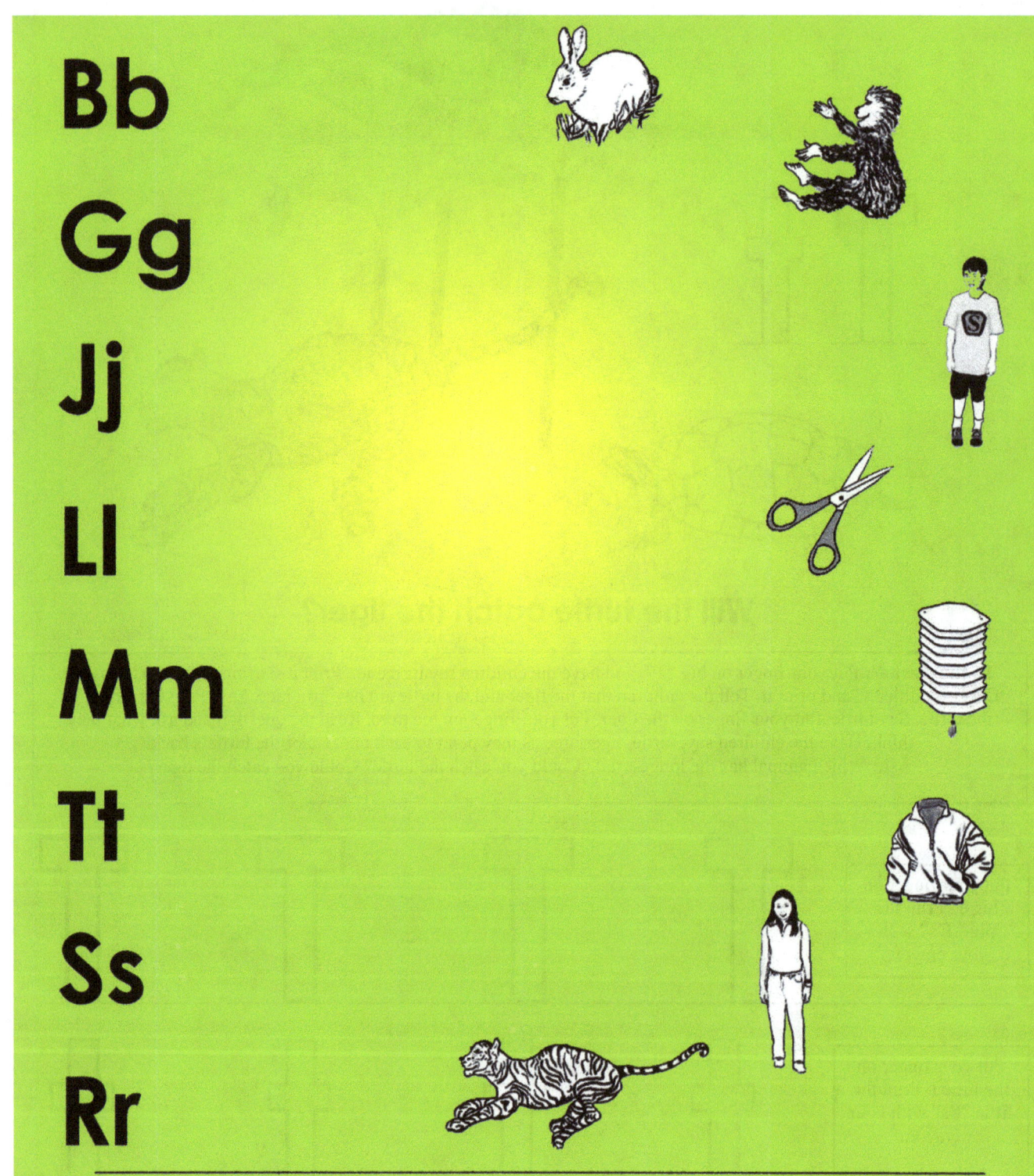

The Alphabet 2 - Student Reader

LESSON 20 CONTINUED

To the teacher: Review the verses from Page 59, having the children repeat them several times. Read this verse to them, they'll enjoy repeating the chorus. Say: Put your finger on the wooden boat. Color its sails. Put your finger on the top bunk. Color the pillows. Put your finger on the picture. Color the sea lion. Put your finger on the boy's legs. Color his socks. Review the meaning of "here" and "there".

My wooden boat's a Chinese junk, It hangs above my brother's bunk.

My boats are here, My boats are there, My little boats are everywhere.

Color all the sails.

The Alphabet 2 - Student Reader

LESSON 21

Objectives – to teach: the symbol name and sound for short Uu – identifying the initial short Uu in words – vocabulary – sentence structure – sentence comprehension – identifying visual differences – identifying auditory differences – following oral directions – reviewing a story – listening to and saying a new verse - printing

Umbrellas in the Rain

To the teacher: Tell the children that it's raining so all the animals need their umbrellas. **Say:** Put your finger on the big umbrella and say "umbrella". Repeat for the smallest umbrellas, the tiger's, the kangaroo's, the baby kangaroo's, the bird's. Put your finger on big "U", print it starting at the top. Repeat for little "u".
Count the umbrellas. Color the smallest umbrellas.
Ask: Do animals have umbrellas?

Print the big "U"s with your crayon. Start at the top.

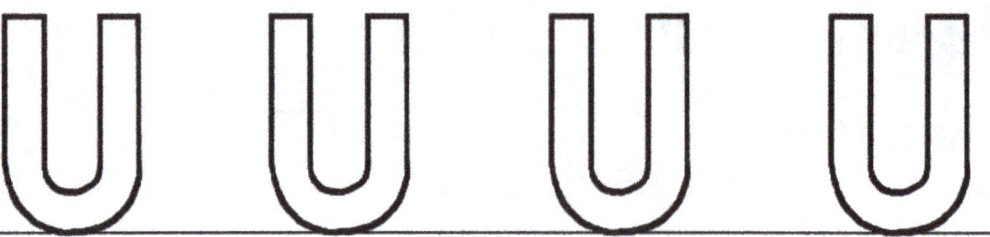

The Alphabet 2 - Student Reader

LESSON 21 CONTINUED

Print the little "u's" with your crayon.

Put your finger on the turtle - umbrella. Follow the dots to make the pictures.

Put your finger on the pictures and the letter and say their names – kite, umbrella, moon, Tt, turtle, tree, tiger, jack-in-the-box.

Draw a line from the pictures that start with Tt, to the letter Tt.

T t

The Alphabet 2 - Student Reader

LESSON 21 CONTINUED

Another boat is made of tin,
Its sides are strong but very thin.

My boats are here,
My boats are there,
My little boats are everywhere.

To the teacher: Read the first two verses from Pages 59 and 62 to the children. Have them say them with you, especially the chorus. Read this verse and the chorus. Have them put their fingers on the: sea picture, Chinese junk, top bunk, pillow, bottom bunk, boy, plastic boat and tin boat. Tell them the tin boat is on a shelf. Have them say the verses with you several times.

Ask: Do you have a boat? What color is your boat? Does your boat have a sail?

Give directions such as: Color the boy's socks brown, color the tin boat red…

Circle the boats that have sails. Draw some water under the boats with your blue crayon.

Point to the letters and say their names. Circle the letters that are the same.

The Alphabet 2 - Student Reader

LESSON 22

Objectives – to teach: the symbol name and sound for Vv – identifying the initial Vv in words – vocabulary – sentence structure – sentence comprehension - identifying visual differences – identifying auditory differences – following oral directions – reviewing a story - listening to and saying a new verse –- printing.

Will you be my valentine?

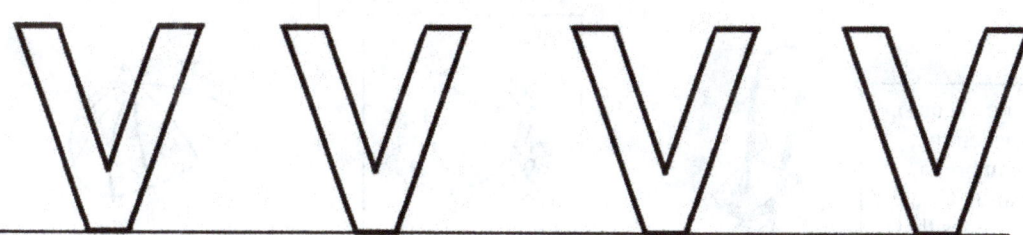

Print the big "V's" with your crayon, starting at the top.

Have the children put their finger on big "V" and say its name.
Repeat for little "v". They are to put their finger on the valentine and say valentine, stressing the first sound.
Read "I love you". And explain the question.

To the teacher: The myth about Valentine's day on February 14 tells us that Saint Valentine helped people and showed love to the poor. Today, people celebrate Valentine's Day by giving cards or flowers or chocolates to those they love. Children exchange cards at school and sometimes have a party.
Read the message on the card to the children and the caption below. Have them color the heart red and the space around the lace any color. You might want to have them cut out the card to give to their parents.
Ask: What is your name? What is her name? What is his name? On the back they can print beside To and From.

The Alphabet 2 - Student Reader

LESSON 22 CONTINUED

Print the little "v's" with your crayon.

This is the back of the valentine. Paste this on the back of the valentine if necessary. Some of this can be done at home if there is limited time.

Say: vacuum, valentine, umbrella, violin. Circle the ones that start with Vv.

Ss   **Tt**   **Rr**   **Vv**

Say: Put your finger on the: valentine, scissors, tiger, rabbit. Draw a line from each picture to the letter it starts with.

The Alphabet 2 - Student Reader

LESSON 22 CONTINUED

To the teacher: Read the verses on Pages 59, 62 and 65. Have the children repeat them with you. Read the new verse and point out the paper boats on the shelf. **Ask:** Do you make paper boats? Have the children say the names of all the things in the room while they point to them – picture, Chinese junk, tin boat, book, bunk, pillow, paper boats, shelf, boy, plastic boat. Read the verses with the children several times. Put your finger on the: paper boats, book, top bunk. Color the paper boats, the book, the boy's shirt, the boy's socks, the pillow.

My paper boats
I've made myself,
I like to keep them
on my shelf.

My boats are here,
My boats are there,
My little boats are everywhere.

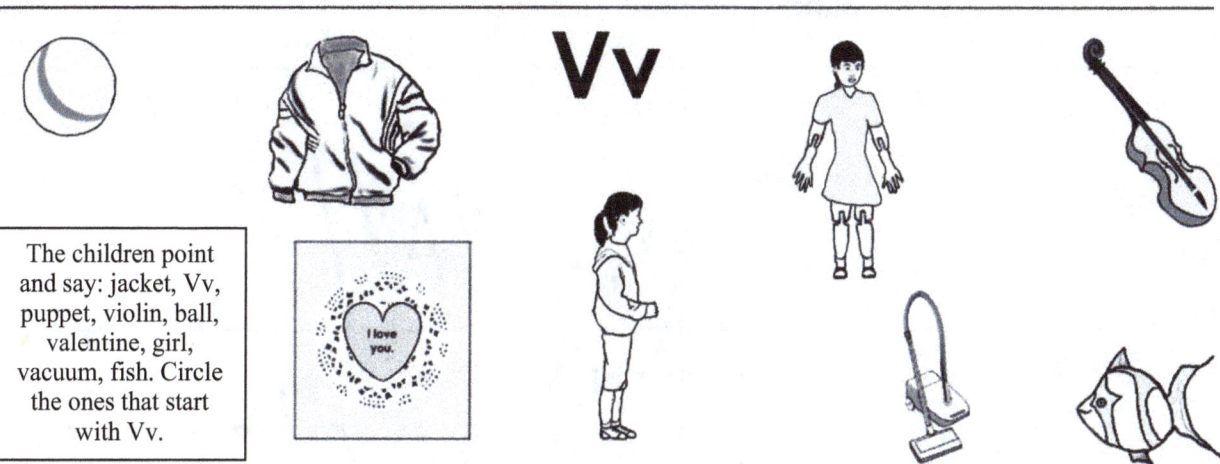

The children point and say: jacket, Vv, puppet, violin, ball, valentine, girl, vacuum, fish. Circle the ones that start with Vv.

LESSON 23

Objectives – to teach: the symbol name and sound for Ww – identifying the initial Ww in words – vocabulary – sentence structure – sentence comprehension - identifying visual differences – identifying auditory differences – matching sounds and symbols - following oral directions - listening to and saying a verse in a new story –- printing.

To the teacher: This woodpecker lives in the forests of North America. It eats small bugs and insects that live in the trees. It has a bright red crest on its head.

Say: Put your finger on the big "W". **Say** W. Print it with your crayon starting at the top. Put your finger on little "w". Print it with your crayon. Put your finger on the picture. **Say**: woodpecker, tree, insects, leaves.

Color the top of the woodpecker's head red. Count the insects with wings. How many did you find?

The woodpecker finds insects in the tree.

Print the big "W's" with your crayon. Start at the top.

Print the little "w's" with your crayon.

The Alphabet 2 - Student Reader

LESSON 23 CONTINUED

To the teacher: The walrus lives on the cold northern ice.
Say: walrus, walrus, sea lion. Circle the one that is different.

Say: W, M, W. Circle the one that is different.

Have the children point to the letters and say their names: Ff, Jj, Ss, Ww, Rr, Uu. Point to the pictures that say their names, stressing the first sound. rabbit, jacket, umbrella, fish, scissors, walrus.
They are to draw lines from each letter to the picture that starts with that sound.

Ff

Jj

Ss

Ww

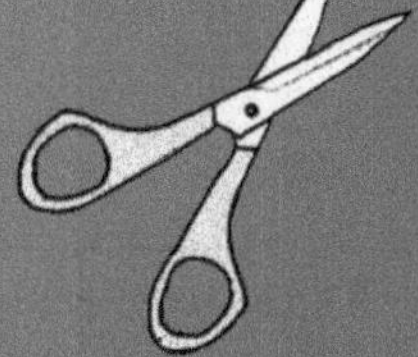

Rr

Uu

LESSON 23 CONTINUED

MAKE BELIEVE

We all could play we're fuzzy bears,
Then roll and tumble on the stairs.

My friends are here,
They've come to play,
They've come to play with me today.

> **To the teacher:** Explain that the children are dressed up as bears. Ask them to decide which are girls and which are boys. One will be unknown. Ask if they ever dress up. Read the verses to them several times.
> **Ask:** Do your friends come to play? How many bear's ears do you see? How many bear's tails? Can you see some bear's teeth? Color three of the friend's faces pink.

Color the bear that is different.

The Alphabet 2 - Student Reader

LESSON 24

Objectives – to teach: the symbol name and sound for Xx – identifying the initial Xx in xylophone – vocabulary – sentence structure – sentence comprehension - identifying visual differences – identifying auditory differences – identifying sounds with symbols - following oral directions – listening to and repeating the story on Page 30 – understanding the new story – repeating the chorus –- printing.

To the teacher: There are only a few words in English where the first letter is Xx. In these, the sound is zz, whereas in words such as "exit" and "fox" the letter name is sounded.
Introduce the example below and move on to the other letters. Have them print the x's starting at the top.

She plays the xylophone.

To the teacher: Tell the children that she makes music on the xylophone. **Say:** Put your finger on the xylophone, lady, big X, little X.. Print big X with your crayon. Print little X with your crayon. Color the lady's arms.

Print the big "X's" with your crayon. Start at the top.				

Print the little "x's" with your crayon.				

Have the children point to each picture as they say: elephant, xylophone, dinosaur. Circle the one that starts with Xx.

 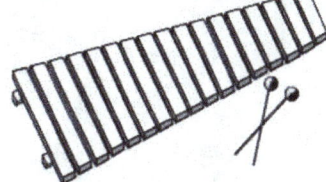 

The Alphabet 2 - Student Reader

LESSON 24 CONTINUED

The children are to say the name as they put their finger on the: Gg, Kk, Nn, Oo, Pp, Rr, Tt, Uu, Aa. Then they say the picture name stressing the first sound, as they put their finger on the: tiger, rabbit, girl, umbrella, kite apple, necklace, panda, octopus. They draw lines from each letter to the picture that starts with that sound.

The Alphabet 2 - Student Reader

LESSON 24 CONTINUED

My friends are here,
They've come to play,
They've come to play with me today.

To the teacher: Have the children point to the Indians. Review. Read the verse. Repeat. **Say**: Put your finger on: the path, the Indian's boots, their feather hats, their jackets, their pants. Color: the Indian's boots, their jackets.

Help the Clown find his way home!

Tell the children to use their crayons to find the Indian's path home. They can't cross any of the lines.

The Alphabet 2 - Student Reader

LESSON 25

Objectives – to teach: the symbol name and sound for Yy – identifying the initial Yy in words – vocabulary – sentence structure – sentence comprehension - identifying visual differences – identifying auditory differences – identifying sounds with symbols - following oral directions – listening to and repeating the stories understanding the new story – repeating the chorus –- printing.

Would you like to ride on a yak?

To the teacher: Tell the children the yak lives in the high mountains of China and Tibet where it is very cold. It has long hair to keep it warm.
Say: Put your finger on the yak, boy, girl, big Y, little y. **Say** Yy. Print the big Y with your crayon. Start at the top. Print the little y with your crayon.
Color the boy's shirt yellow. Color the girl's shirt blue. Color the yak's horns brown.

Print the big "Y's" with your crayon starting at the top.

Print the little "Y's" with your crayon.

The Alphabet 2 - Student Reader

LESSON 25 CONTINUED

The children are to listen to the first sound of the color names. When the color name is called they are to put their finger on its first letter. When they have the letter, they are to color the star beside it the color that was called. Call these color names one at a time. The children will need help identifying the right letters.
green, yellow, blue, purple, white, brown, red, pink. Note that there are two b's and two p's.

Before starting have the children color the star yellow.
The children point to the pictures as you **say:** yellow, yak, clown. Stress the first sound.
Color the ones that start with Yy.

Gg    **Ww**

Bb    **Yy**

Pp    **Bb**

Pp    **Rr**

76   The Alphabet 2 - Student Reader

LESSON 25 CONTINUED

We might all be such funny clowns,
With boys in hats, and girls in gowns.

My friends are here,
They've come to play,
They've come to play with me today.

To the teacher: Review the verses on pages 71 and 74, having the children say them with you several times. Read the new verse and have the children join in on the chorus. Ask again if their friends come to play.
Also: Have you ever seen a clown? Would you like to be a clown? Say: Put your finger on - the boy clowns, the girl clowns, the girl's gowns, the umbrella, the clown's hats. Color the girl's gowns.

Say: Put your finger on: the girl – her dress – her tights – her mouth – her shoes – her eyes – her nose.

Put your finger on your mouth – eyes – nose.

How many fingers does she have?
Color her tights orange and black.
Color the spots on her dress yellow.
Color her shoes orange.

The Alphabet 2 - Student Reader

LESSON 26

Objectives – to teach: the symbol name and sound for Zz – identifying the initial Zz – vocabulary – sentence structure – sentence comprehension - identifying visual differences – identifying auditory differences – identifying sounds with symbols - following oral directions – listening to and repeating the story on Pages 71, 74 and 79 – understanding the new story – repeating the chorus –- printing.

The zebras are eating grass.

To the teacher: Tell the student that the zebras are eating grass. **Say:** Put your finger on the: zebras, grass, mountain, big Z, little z. Print big "Z" with your crayon. Print little "z".

Print the big "Z's" with your crayon. Start at the top.

Print the little "z's" with your crayon.

78 The Alphabet 2 - Student Reader

LESSON 26 CONTINUED

The children are to say the letter name as they put their finger on the: Pp, Nn, Ii, Ww, Zz, Yy, Ff, Ss. Then they say the picture names stressing the first sound, as they put their finger on: Indian, zebra, woodpecker, panda, fish scissors, necklace, yak. They are to draw lines from each letter to the picture that starts with the sound.

The Alphabet 2 - Student Reader

LESSON 26 CONTINUED

**To be good jugglers would be fun
We'd throw the balls and catch and run.**

**My friends are here
They've come to play
They've come to play with me today.**

Trace the dots with your crayon to make the picture.

To the teacher: Review the verses on pages 71, 74, and 77, having the children say them with you several times. Read the new verse and have the children join in on the chorus. Ask again if their friends come to play.
Also: Have you ever seen a juggler? Would you like to be a juggler? **Say:** Put your finger on the boy at the top. How many balls does he have? How many girl jugglers do you see? How many balls does the Indian boy have? Color the Indian's boots black. Color the girl bear brown. Color the spots on the girl's dress.

The Alphabet 2 - Student Reader

ESL Alphabet - 2
M - Z

The monkey sits on a mushroom under the moon.

Practice Book

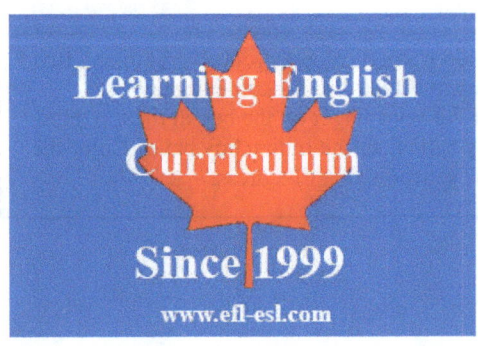

LESSON 13

M m

monkey

M

m

moon

Student Workbook

25

LESSON 13 CONTINUED

moon

M M M M

Draw yourself with a moon.

m m m m

26 Student Workbook

LESSON 14

N n

N

necklace

n

nest

Student Workbook

27

LESSON 14 CONTINUED

narwhale

n n n n n n

Draw a narwhale in the water.

N N N N N

28
Student Workbook

LESSON 15

Oo

otter

octopus

29

Student Workbook

LESSON 15 CONTINUED

Draw what you eat.

osprey

30 Student Workbook

LESSON 16

P p

P

p

panda

pig

LESSON 16 CONTINUED

pelican

pelican

Draw fishes for the pelican to eat.

LESSON 17

Q

quail

q

queen

LESSON 17 CONTINUED

Q Q Q

q q q

You draw a beautiful queen!

She is a queen.

queen

34 Student Workbook

LESSON 18

Rr

R _____ rabbit

_____ rhinoceros

r

35

LESSON 18 CONTINUED

rabbit

R R

R R

r r r

r r r

You draw a rabbit.

rabbit

LESSON 19

S s

S

sea lion

S

scissors

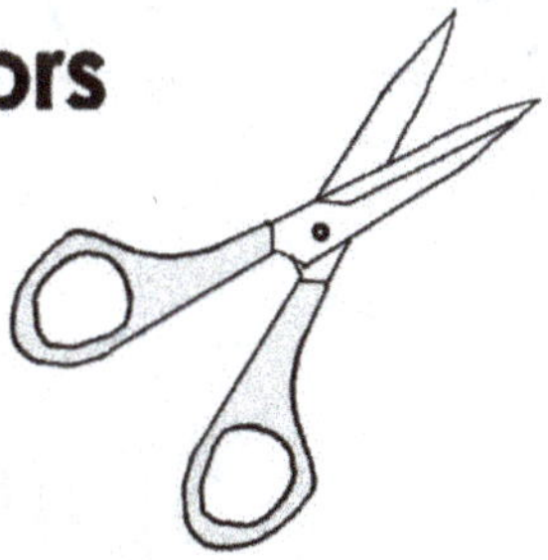

Student Workbook

37

LESSON 19 CONTINUED

You draw a **big** spider.

spider

LESSON 20

T t

turtle

T

tiger

t

Student Workbook

LESSON 20 CONTINUED

You draw a **big** turtle and a **little** turtle.

turtle

LESSON 21

U u

U

umbrella

U

umbrella

LESSON 21 CONTINUED

umbrellas

You draw an umbrella.

umbrella

U U U u u u

LESSON 22

Vv

V

van

V

vacuum

LESSON 22 CONTINUED

valentine

valentine
_____
_____
_____
_____

You draw a valentine.

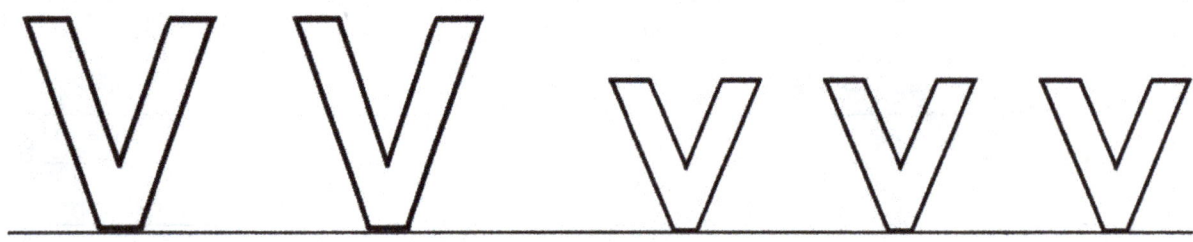

LESSON 23

W w

w _____ walrus

w _____ woodpecker

LESSON 23 CONTINUED
walrus

You color the big walrus and the little walrus.

walrus

LESSON 24

X x

xylophone

X

X

47
Student Workbook

LESSON 24 CONTINUED
xylophone

Color the xylophone.

xylophone

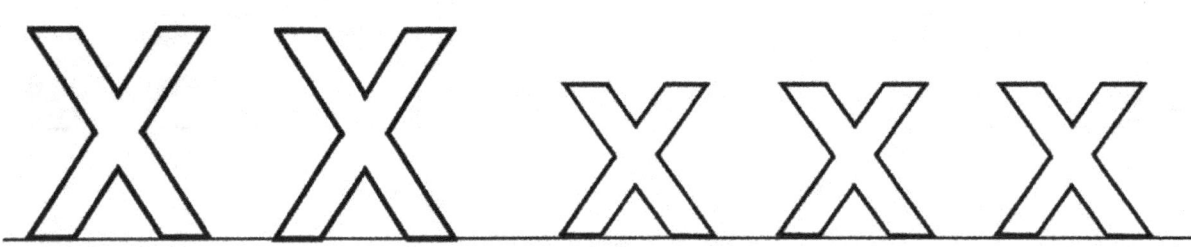

LESSON 25

Y y

Y

yak

y

49
Student Workbook

LESSON 25 CONTINUED
yacht

You color the yacht.

Y Y y y y

50 Student Workbook

LESSON 26

zebra

Z z

Z

z

LESSON 26 CONTINUED
ZOO

You are at the zoo!

ZOO

ESL Alphabet - 2
M - Z

The monkey sits on a mushroom under the moon.

Teacher Guide

Daisy Stocker M. Ed.
Dr. George Stocker D.D.S.

Learning English Curriculum
Since 1999
www.efl-esl.com

BOOK 1B: GAME 1. Use between Lessons 1 and 14. Only use the pictures that have been used in the lessons to date. Photocopy the pages and cut out the pictures. Give each student a small piece of paper. The teacher holds up one picture, and the students who can say the one word name, of the item on the card, gets a stamp on their paper. This game is best played with a small group.

GAME 2. For this game the teacher distributes the cut out pictures. The teacher then calls out the captions to be found beneath the pictures on the page below. The student(s) who has (have) the corresponding picture is to hold up their picture.

Teacher Guide

49

LESSONS 1 TO 14

LESSONS 1 TO 14

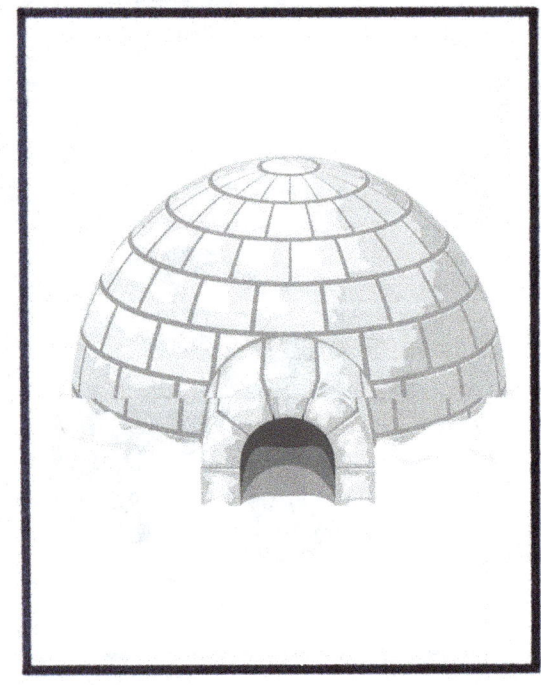

LESSONS 1 TO 14

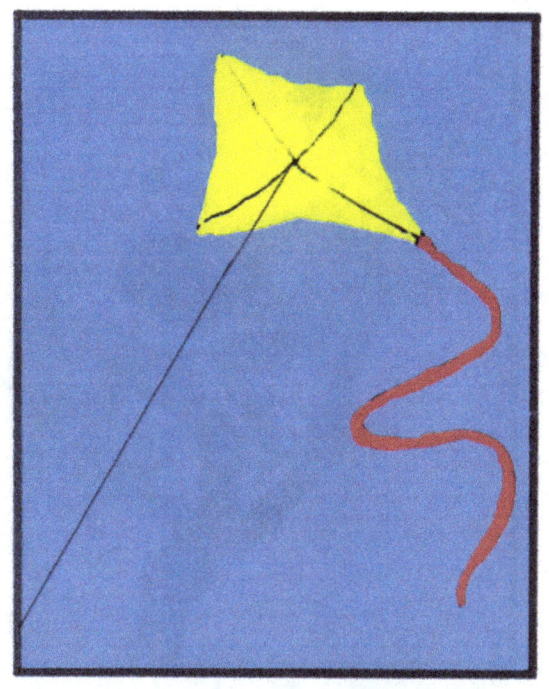
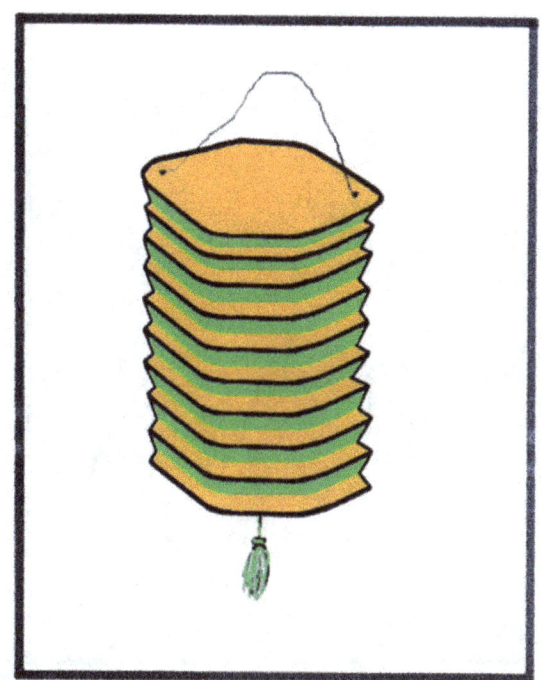

LESSONS 1 TO 14

LESSONS 1 TO 14

LESSONS 1 TO 14

Teacher Guide

GAME 3   MODIFIED BINGO

Give each student one Bingo card from pages 59 to 68.
Most of the pictures and the captions are taken straight from the lessons.
Several of the captions will contain a new word.
The students are not expected to know all the captions on the first or second time through the game.
Rather, it is a learning process, so that after a few games, the students will be able to respond quickly and accurately.
Help the students at first, and encourage them to help each other.

Bingo Captions
These are shown with the corresponding pictures on Page 57.

The monkey sits on the mushroom under the moon.
The narwhale has a long nose.
The octopus lives in the sea.
The pandas live in the trees.
The queen is feeding the ducks.
Cock-a-doodle-doo! Good morning to you.
The spider made a web in the tree.
Will the turtle catch the tiger?
Umbrellas in the rain.

Enrichment Captions
Use these when the children are successful with the captions above.
These are shown with the corresponding pictures on Page 58.

The black and white bear is in the tree.
The spider spun a web.
The monkey is looking at the moon.
The ducks like to eat.
The animals have umbrellas.
The tiger and the turtle run.
The narwhale is in the water.
The rooster says, "Good morning".
The octopus has many legs.

Teacher Guide

GAME 3   MODIFIED BINGO
Teacher's Copy

The pandas live in the trees.	The spider made a web in the tree.	The monkey sits on the mushroom under the moon.
The queen is feeding the ducks.	Umbrellas in the rain.	Will the turtle catch the tiger?
The narwhale has a long nose.	Cock-a-doodle-doo! Good morning to you.	The octopus lives in the sea.

BOOK 1B   GAME 3   MODIFIED BINGO
Enrichment Copy

Teacher Guide

GAME 3   MODIFIED BINGO
Card 1

Teacher Guide

GAME 3 MODIFIED BINGO

Card 2

Teacher Guide

GAME 3   MODIFIED BINGO
Card 3

Teacher Guide

GAME 3   MODIFIED BINGO

Card 4

GAME 3   MODIFIED BINGO

Card 5

Teacher Guide

GAME 3   MODIFIED BINGO

Card 6

Teacher Guide

GAME 3 MODIFIED BINGO

Card 7

Teacher Guide

65

GAME 3   MODIFIED BINGO

Card 8

Teacher Guide

GAME 3   MODIFIED BINGO

Card 9

Teacher Guide

67

GAME 3   MODIFIED BINGO

Card 10

Teacher Guide

TEST   **Name** _____

Part 1: Say the name of each picture as the children draw the line to match the letter to the initial sound. : spider, monkey, turtle, queen, umbrella, zebra, valentine, rabbit. **Marks:** Part1: 8   Part 2: 8   Part 3: 4   Total: 20 marks

Uu

Ss

Mm

Vv

Tt

Qq

Zz

Rr

Teacher Guide   i

TEST CONTINUED   Name _____

Part 2: As the children work say the name of each color in any order: red, green, purple, white, yellow, black, blue, orange. The children are to listen, find the letter with that color's initial sound and color the hat beside it.

Yy    Pp

Rr    Bb

Bb    Oo

Gg    Ww

Part 3: Say the alphabet names. Say the names of the picture in each line – rabbit, yellow, yak/ necklace, nest, tiger/ woodpecker, pig, walrus/ octopus, otter, umbrella/ The children are to circle the pictures that start with that letter.

Yy

Nn

Ww

Oo

GLOSSARY

Aa	Hh
above	help
all	here
along	hers
always	him
animal	home
another	horn
arm	Ii
as	if
Bb	I've
because	Jj
bed	jacket
beside	juggler
biggest	jump
bird	junk
boat	Kk
boot	keep
brother	knee
bunk	Ll
but	leads
Cc	let
can't	long
chasing	lots
cock-a-doodle-doo	love
come	Mm
could	made
Dd	make
each	me
eat	might
eating	missing
elbow	monkey
everywhere	moon
Ee	morning
feeding	mushroom
fin	my
friend	myself
from	Nn
fun	name
funny	narwhale
fuzzy	necklace
Gg	nest
gown	Oo
grass	octopus
Hh	of
hair	once
hang	one

Teacher Guide

71

GLOSSARY

Pp	Tt
panda	they've
pants	thin
paper	throw
path	tiger
pencil	time
perhaps	tin
picture	today
pig	toes
plastic	tree
play	tried
please	tumble
pond	turtle
pony	**Uu**
puppet	umbrella
Qq	under
queen	until
Rr	up
rabbit	upon
rain	us
ran	using
ride	**Vv**
roll	valentine
rooster	very
run	walking
Ss	walrus
sail	web
scissors	we'll
sea	we're
shelf	when
shoe	who'll
side	will
sit	with
so	wooden
some	woodpecker
spider	**Xx**
spot	xylophone
stairs	**Yy**
started	yak
strong	**Zz**
such	zebra
sun	zoo
Tt	
tail	
teeth	
then	

Children's ESL Graphic Novels

ESL COMIC BOOKS – A NEW APPROACH
These books offer an oral approach for young ESL / EFL students.

They contain high interest stories, written in the graphics novel format that children love. This is very suitable for supplementary study, home school, as well as for summer camps.

JAMBO GOES TO THE MOON – GRAPHIC NOVEL VERSION

Jambo has a very smart brain, that continually gets him into trouble. He is caught and sent to the moon, where even his smart brain is challenged, and all he wants is to go back to his jungle. The vocabulary learned is reinforced by 4 Picture Bingo games.

Includes

- Word Bingo Games and Crossword Puzzles.
- 3 books in 1 -- Teacher's Guide, Storybook and Workbook.
- Print as many copies as required

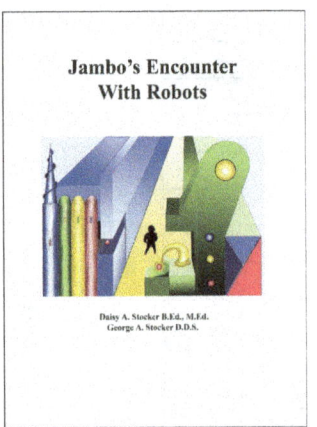

JAMBO'S ENCOUNTER WITH ROBOTS – GRAPHIC NOVEL VERSION

Jambo goes to sleep and mysteriously wakes up in the Robot City! Here he learns the value of good friends. Jambo uses his very smart brain to get back to the Jungle.

Includes

- Word Bingo Games and Crossword Puzzles.
- 3 books in 1 -- Teacher's Guide, Storybook and Workbook.
- Print as many copies as required

THE MYSTERY OF THE SECRET CODE – GRAPHIC NOVEL VERSION

This edition of The Mystery of the Secret Code is written in a graphics novel format for English Second Language students. The story is adapted from the ESL Storybook, of the same name.

This ESL Mystery Book is appropriate for students aged 8 to 12. It stresses listening, understanding and speaking. The children are encouraged to suggest solutions to the problems that the storybook characters encounter and express their creative ideas.

Includes
- Word Bingo Games and Crossword Puzzles.
- 3 books in 1 -- Teacher's Guide, Storybook and Workbook.

https://efl-esl.com/esl-graphic-novels-for-children/

Complete Teen Adult ESL Curriculum

Module 1 – Beginners

Module 2 – High Beginner

Module 3 – Intermediate

Module 4 – Advanced

Complete ESL Curriculum for all Levels

- 160 Lessons
- Over 1400 pages of ESL activities, lesson plans, games and more
- Each module includes, Student Reader, Student Workbook and Teacher Guide
- Tests and Reviews with every level and section
- Ready for the classroom

Purchase each module separately or all 4 together for 25% off

https://www.efl-esl.com/curriculum/

www.ingramcontent.com/pod-product-compliance
Lightning Source LLC
Chambersburg PA
CBHW080347170426
43194CB00014B/2714